# Inner Strength, Outer Success

## A savvy gal's guide to financial empow(er)ment

### Beth Burns, C.P.C.

Illustrations by Karen Light

*published by*
**the (er) factor**
Chicago, Illinois
www.erisinher.com
www.innerstrengthoutersuccess.com

Copyright © 2018 by Beth Burns, C.P.C.

ISBN: 978-0-69212-905-0

Printed in the United States of America

my message aims to inspire women
to be more financially empow(er)ed.

(er) is in her ... find your (er) inside®

www.innerstrengthoutersuccess.com

# Contents

INTRODUCTION:
My Financial Wake-up Call . . . . . . . . . . . . 1

The Importance of Financial
Empow(er)ment . . . . . . . . . . . . . . . . . . . . . 5

Have Goals . . . . . . . . . . . . . . . . . . . . . . . . 9

Pay Yourself First . . . . . . . . . . . . . . . . . . 15

Credit Score, Credit Cards,
and Interest Rates . . . . . . . . . . . . . . . . . 19

Wealth vs. Stuff . . . . . . . . . . . . . . . . . . . . 25

Create a Budget . . . . . . . . . . . . . . . . . . . . 31

Conclusion . . . . . . . . . . . . . . . . . . . . . . . . 39

APPENDIX:
Basic Terms of Investing . . . . . . . . . . . . . 43

References. . . . . . . . . . . . . . . . . . . . . . . . . 51

About the Author. . . . . . . . . . . . . . . . . . . . 53

# INTRODUCTION:
# My Financial Wake-up Call

**Others don't empow(er) us; we empow(er) ourselves.** If we want to change an outcome, we must change how we respond. It is a change in our behavior, which is fueled inside of us, that will result in changing outcomes; thus, the meaning of the phrase *(er) is in her . . . find your (er) inside*®. This sounds simple, but change takes constant and continual effort. Others can assist us, but it is up to us to plant and nurture the seed inside of us of what we truly want.

If we wish to be more financially empow(er)ed, we must change how we relate to money daily. We can receive money from various sources, but, ultimately, learning how to manage money to receive the desired outcome is financial empow(er)ment. Is our spending thoughtful and strategic, or is it random and not well planned? We have to learn how to control our money and not let our money control us.

The essence of financial empow(er)ment is controlling the flow of money. Our saving and spending behaviors are fundamental to this flow. Gratification is deferred yet rewarded when we save, while spending fuels immediate indulgence. A balance between the two is needed to master financial empow(er)ment. Saving is so much harder than spending, but saving yields lasting results. We are not born with the ability to manage our finances; these skills are learned. The earlier we adopt these skills, the earlier we can lay a strong financial foundation, which can be pivotal to success in life.

## My Early Relationship with Money

I have always been a saver. I learned early in my childhood the value of saving money. My parents started a savings account for me when I was a toddler. Any checks or cash gifts I received for my birthdays would be deposited in my savings account for college. With every deposit, I would witness the ever-growing account balance, with interest! This discipline taught me that with patience, the number would increase. This effort was my introduction to what having wealth felt like, and it was a great feeling. Even though my savings was small, it taught me an invaluable lesson about material items and wealth. With patience and perseverance, money will grow while material items will lose their value and usefulness. When I would get my allowance as an adolescent, I would put my money away like a squirrel preparing for a long, cold winter. I only spent my allowance on things that were really important to me.

## My Financial Wake-up Call

When I started my professional career in 1986, I did not immediately begin contributing to my employer-sponsored long-term savings program, nor did I start saving for a rainy day. This was the first time in my life I had a little bit of financial freedom, and I wanted to enjoy. Why worry? I was well educated, had a good job, and worked for a large, well-established company.

After obtaining my MBA in 1993, where I was indoctrinated with the concept of compounded growth, I wised up and immediately enrolled in my employer-sponsored long-term savings program. I was now saving long term, in addition to putting a little aside for vacations and unplanned expenses. Boom, it hit! Thirteen years into my career, I faced two bouts of unemployment. I was laid off from my job in 1999 and then again in 2003. I have two degrees: a BS in engineering and an MBA from a highly ranked graduate program. I never thought it would happen to me, but it did.

With only two and a half years between the occurrences, I did not have much time to financially recover. My state unemployment benefits were my only source of income both times. During my fourteen-month unemployment, the state benefits ceased after twelve months. State unemployment benefits are not infinite. I was fortunate that my unemployment check covered a large percentage of my mortgage. I was lucky that my mortgage was reasonable, so I was able to maintain my house during unemployment. At the time when I purchased my home, my monthly mortgage was less than 25 percent of my monthly gross income.

A standard rule of thumb for lenders is that your monthly housing payment (principal, interest, taxes, and insurance) should not exceed 28 percent of gross income.[1]

I used the small savings I had accumulated to pay my mortgage and bills for household expenses like utilities. All other expenses were paid for with a credit card. A credit card can be a costly form of currency. I never touched what I had contributed to my employer-sponsored long-term savings plan during my unemployment. I still wanted my money working for me, even though I was not working and could not contribute to the plan.

## Introduction: My Financial Wake-up Call

When I secured a job after my periods of unemployment, my first goal was to pay off all the credit card debt. Next, I had to diligently save to rebuild my spare cash account and then continue saving for retirement. Those two-plus years of unemployment put me further behind in my retirement savings than I already was given that I did not start contributing early in my career. Now that I was back to work, I needed to maximize my contributions. To accomplish my savings goals, I would have to rethink my spending. Unemployment was indeed a learning experience; it was a financial wake-up call. I became much wiser with my spending and saving habits, which ultimately put me on the path of sound fiscal responsibility.

I wrote this book because I want others to learn from both my successes and failures. I want to share the strategies that I integrated into my life. Regardless of your age, there is always room to incorporate new strategies into your life. If you have bad habits, it is never too late to retrain your brain to react differently. My wish is that my fellow gals be savvy as it relates to financial empow(**er**)ment. We have the power; it's up to us to incorporate change into our daily lives.

**Inner strength** leads to **outer success**.

# The Importance of Financial Empow(er)ment

**Do you want to be happier?** We all strive to be happier in life, and we are happier when we achieve the goals we set for ourselves. Often our financial situation becomes an impediment to embarking on our goals and can be a source of stress. Being good stewards of our money takes discipline. Every moment of every day we are faced with decisions on how we will part with our hard-earned money. Financial discipline will determine how and when we decide to part with our money. This discipline needs to become routine so that it does not require much thought or effort, and does not cause a feeling of denial but rather one of liberation.

The lack of financial stability can be debilitating, as it impacts so many aspects of our lives. The earlier in life we begin focusing on our financial shrewdness, the better off we are later in life. But it is never too late to adopt sound financial discipline, regardless of your phase in life. Financial security will pave the road to being happier. Financial discipline comprises many aspects. Paramount in our minds should be our life's goals. To support our goals, we need to save money to address both short- and long-term objectives. We should establish a routine of saving monthly and adjust our lifestyles to live on less than what we earn. It is critical to understand the importance of having a high credit score and how interest rates can have a significant impact on how much we ultimately spend on the items we purchase.

If we genuinely want to create wealth, we must limit our spending on things with little long-term value. The foundation of financial stability is creating and sticking to a budget. Like any aspect of empow(er)ment, financial discipline takes diligence and tenacity.

It is especially imperative for women to concern ourselves and become savvier as it relates to saving and investing. More than ever, women are heads of the household, both financially and figuratively. Saving is especially imperative for women for the following reasons:

$ On average women live longer than men. Therefore, we will need more money in retirement than men.

$ On average women make less money and receive fewer salary increases than men, so we have less to potentially save or invest.

$ Women tend to lose more income following a divorce than men.

$ When we do invest, women are typically less aggressive in their investment strategies. Thus, long-term return is lower.

$ Women are more inclined to change jobs or work part-time more often than men, disrupting our income stream.

$ On average women spend less time in the workforce than men due to time off for child-rearing, as well as a host of other reasons, and therefore make less money than men over the span of our careers.

## The Importance of Financial Empow(er)ment

Our financial security is up to us. We cannot relinquish the control of our finances to others or think that others will create a comfortable nest egg or safety net on which we can rely. We need to get involved, initiate the conversation about our finances, understand the details of what's going on with our money, and make changes if necessary. We cannot let our lack of financial prowess be a speed bump on our ultimate road to happiness. We owe it to ourselves to be more engaged in our financial security.

Our **financial security** is up to us.

# Have Goals

**We all have goals. What is life without them?** Goals are why we work. Some of our goals don't cost a thing, but most goals do have some financial implication. We must detail those goals and keep them front and center daily. We cannot allow the more significant long-term goals to get pushed to the back of our minds because small things are monopolizing our attention. We must create a vision of what we want our lives to look like now and in the future. By visualizing those images, we will remain focused. Allow me to share some of the goals I contemplate annually:

$ Remain physically active as much as possible.

$ Retire before age sixty-five.

$ Add one or two on-trend pieces to my wardrobe from the current season.

$ Travel to someplace I have never been (for example, Paris, Illinois, or Paris, France).

$ Bike or hike in the mountains of the desert or relax on a lovely beach.

$ Add a new piece of furniture or some other upgrade to my home.

The goals above are not in any particular order because how I prioritize these goals changes every year and I cannot address them all every year. For instance, in a year that I want to take a big international trip, I may have to forgo a hiking trip and a new item for my home. In a year that I have to make a significant home improvement, my vacations are closer to home. In a year that I am looking to get into great physical shape because my clothes are getting a bit too tight, I will invest in a personal trainer and postpone the beach trip until I can rock an awesome bathing suit.

At the beginning of each year, I lay out the details of my goals and how I will make them happen. I modify my spending to achieve these goals. This list stays at the forefront of my mind all the time so that unnecessary purchases will not tempt me. For every nonessential purchase I make today, there is a trade-off between achieving a longer-term goal tomorrow, so I spend wisely.

## Physically Active

Because I want to remain physically active, a gym membership will always be part of my life. I have been a member of both the very upscale and the more modestly priced health clubs. Depending on the priorities for that year, I will work some type of gym membership into my budget. In the last couple of years, travel has been high on the list, so I have been a member of the no-frills neighborhood gym.

I own a bicycle, and when weather permits, you will see me enjoying Chicago's lakefront path on my two wheels or walking on my two feet. Remaining physically active has the added benefit of keeping my weight in check, dramatically slowing the spread of my hips. Many of the well-made timeless clothes that I purchased years ago still fit, thus saving money in the long run.

## Retiring Early

**One of** my lifelong goals is to retire before age sixty-five so that I can travel the world. **I would** like to retire early while I still have the energy to enjoy my travels to the fullest. **I love** being active, and in retirement, I would enjoy living in a climate that will allow me **to enjoy** the outdoors daily. The Chicago climate keeps me indoors much too often for my active appetite. The mountains in the southwest desert or the warm breezes of beachfront living is my vision of my life in the future.

I knew early in my career that I did not want to work forever. Working is just one of the many acts in the play called life. I often ponder living expenses in retirement. A mortgage payment is usually one of the more expensive items in our monthly budget. Before retirement, my goal is to have a property free of debt so that I can live without that monthly expense. When possible, I contribute additional dollars to my mortgage principal to accelerate payoff. I don't want the stress of allocating limited retirement dollars to rent or mortgage. I wish to have more money to play during my retirement years.

## A Fashionable Wardrobe

Having the most updated wardrobe drifts to the bottom of my list because fashion trends change too much. The investment to be the best dressed is not my priority. My mother was a master tailor, and she taught me how to sew when I was child. My mom would make matching outfits for my sisters and me and suits for my dad. She demonstrated to me the construction of impeccable clothing, so I tend to lean toward quality versus quantity.

When I started my career, I would make basic skirts to wear to work. I like beautiful clothes, but I don't want to spend an excessive amount on my daily wardrobe. I don't mind purchasing used clothing, so I often shop at consignment shops and other places that sell fabulous used items. I also love art-fair fare as it offers uniqueness at a reasonable price. In short, I have always been very strategic about what I purchase when it comes to clothes, and I ultimately conceived of what I call my style template.

## My Style Template

For so many of us, a budget deficit will be generated around creating a fantastic wardrobe. There are some strategies that can be employed to build a lovely wardrobe without overspending. You must be very focused regarding your purchases, and these three strategies will help:

First, **understand your body type.** All clothes look good on hangers, but most of us are not shaped like hangers. Proportionally I am a pear shape. I have larger hips and thighs, and I'm smaller on the top and have a long torso.

Second, **recognize the style of clothes that flatter your figure.** Everyone does not look good in everything; determine your template style given your body shape. For my body type, I prefer an A-line dress over a two-piece suit, as the bottom is always tricky to fit. An added bonus is that a stunning dress is much cheaper than a two-piece suit. Also, there is no need to purchase a coordinating blouse for a dress like I would with a two-piece suit. Additionally, dresses are much easier to pack and take up less space when traveling.

Given my pear shape, the bottom half of my body is not that of a runway model, so my wardrobe includes very few pairs of blue jeans or dress pants. My choice for bottoms is a nice thick pair of stretch pants or long stretch skirt for daily wear and running leggings for my weekend wear. When I discover a great quality pair of stretch pants, I will purchase the same brand of pants in black, brown, blue, etc. My bottoms become the background for the more selective items like cute tops, jackets, and blazers, and/or boots and shoes. I refer to this part of my strategy as Tops and Toes! We can all take a page out of the Steve Jobs book of fashion; he wore a black turtleneck with jeans daily.

Third, **avoid browsing in clothing stores.** When shopping, I head directly to the racks with the things that are key to my wardrobe, bypassing all the other items.

## Travel

I love traveling, so I always made it a priority in my life. When I was younger, my travel was exploring the U.S. or spending a long weekend visiting a friend in another state. As time has passed, my travel goals have elevated. A couple of years ago, I ventured to Zambia for a two-week safari, and recently I indulged in an adventure to hike a portion of the Inca Trail to see Machu Picchu. And while in South America, I experienced the wonders of the Galápagos Islands on a cruise. I now think about where I would like to travel next year, maybe Bali, maybe Nepal, or perhaps India, as I have never visited Asia. When I vacation, my wardrobe is basic, often purchased used or from discount stores. My wardrobe is underpriced; the memories are priceless.

Take the time to outline your own goals, review your strategy often, reprioritize if necessary, and continue to strive for what you honestly desire. Do not fall prey to the images and narratives of life subscribed to by others. When you focus on the greater objectives in life, the small things fade away and don't matter as much, especially when a big item can be checked off your list. It is a wonderful feeling when the perceived intangible becomes tangible.

## Only you can make it happen. Turn your dreams into reality!

## To Do:

1. Create a list of short-term and long-term goals and prioritize. Review your goals regularly and strategize regarding the trade-offs that will need to be incorporated into your daily routine. **My goals are:**

   _____

   _____

   _____

   _____

2. Given my body type, I will focus my shopping for clothes on the follow items:

   _____

   _____

   _____

3. Create a vision board so that you can stay focused on your goals. To create a vision board, collect pictures and images that represent your goals. Paste or tape them on heavy stock paper or poster board. Place it somewhere you will be able to see it daily so that you can remain focused on your goals.

# Pay Yourself First

**The concept of *paying yourself first* is a simple one.** As part of your monthly budget, *pay yourself first* by first allocating money to a long-term investment account, either one sponsored by your employer—like a 401(k) or 403(b)—or an individual retirement account (IRA), and second by adding to a personal savings account. Your savings account should be readily accessible and not be invested in anything risky, where there exists a potential for loss. The concept is simple, but often because of other demands in life, this discipline can be challenging. In the long run, you will be thankful if you stick to it.

## Retirement Savings

Do you want to retire from working one day? For most of us, gone are the days of employer-sponsored retirement income and benefits. For my parents, the majority of their retirement income is sourced from their respective pensions. My baby-boomer generation will not have that luxury. I have worked for seven companies in my career, and only two of those companies offered a pension plan, and I stayed with one of those companies just long enough to vest into the program. I was with that organization for seven years, so there are very few dollars in the pension plan for me. By the time I retire and given

inflation, I will be lucky if my monthly pension check will cover a utility bill. Social Security will only offer a small fraction of what I will need to maintain a basic lifestyle. My savings will be my primary source of income in retirement.

Contributing to a long-term savings plan is one of the easiest ways to fund retirement savings. These programs have the additional benefit of being tax-deferred (which means you don't pay taxes until the money is withdrawn), so contributions are made with pre-tax dollars, thus lowering current taxable income. Often employee-sponsored plans are structured in such a way that the employer matches a percentage of the employee contribution, which equals free money. Because contributions are deducted from gross income, there is a forced discipline to budget with take-home pay.

## Personal Savings

Beyond saving for retirement, it is important to have additional cash savings because sh*t happens; it never fails *not* to happen. In life, unexpected expenses occur routinely, so please budget for them. They can range from the happy moments of life like a birthday gift for a friend, to the unfortunate events like a major medical expense, home or car repair, or job loss. It is not realistic to think an unplanned expense will not ensue. In my life, unplanned expenses arise every month without fail.

Establish a routine of putting a little aside monthly. If nothing comes up, congratulations, this is the first step to having a much-needed buffer in the budget. Target additional savings at 3 to 5 percent of take-home pay.

The rule of thumb is to accumulate six months of living expenses in a savings account. I would suggest more because, in my thirty-year career, I have been faced with two prolonged periods of unemployment. It happens to the best of us. This savings account should be used just for emergencies, and the money should be replaced as soon as possible. Treat your savings account just like you treat any other bill you pay monthly. *Pay yourself first* and include it in the budget.

## Do you want to be a millionaire?

You too can be a millionaire. Here's an example: If at twenty years old, you invest $292 monthly (less than $10 per day, the cost of a couple of cups of fancy coffee), you will have $1 million at sixty-five years old, assuming an 7 percent annual return compounded annually. At forty-five years old, you would have to invest $2,033 per month to have $1 million at age sixty-five, assuming an 7 percent annual return compounded annually. It pays to start early, so that you can finish on a high note.

**Patience and perseverance are the keys to financial empow(er)ment.**

**If you start early, it is not an enormous sacrifice. You owe it to yourself!**

## To Do:

1. **Pay yourself first** by contributing to your employer-sponsored retirement saving plan or an IRA. Ensure that you are contributing the amount necessary to receive the maximum tax benefit if contributing to an IRA or another long-term savings program. Please refer to IRS.gov[2] to completely understand contribution limits for the program in which you are investing. If contributing to an employer-sponsored retirement account, inquire about employer match and contribute the amount necessary to maximize the match. If you are not taking advantage of this match, you are leaving money on the table.

2. **Pay yourself first** by creating a little cushion in your budget by saving 3 to 5 percent of your take-home pay each month. It may sting a little now, but you will have peace of mind when something unexpected occurs.

3. To calculate what you need to save monthly to reach your savings goals, go to Investor.gov and scroll down to Financial Planning Tools. Click on COMPOUND INTEREST CALCULATOR AND SAVINGS GOAL CALCULATOR, then click the tab for Savings Goal Calculator.

# Credit Score, Credit Cards, and Interest Rates

**Our credit score is more than a number.** It is a score of credit worthiness. In other words, it represents the potential risk a creditor assumes by lending money to us. It impacts multiple aspects of our lives. The credit score will determine what interest rate we can obtain when applying for credit for a house, car, and revolving credit such as a credit card. Credit scoring is not limited to bank financing but is used by mobile phone companies, insurance companies, landlords, and potential employers. Yes, our credit score can also impact our employment opportunities.

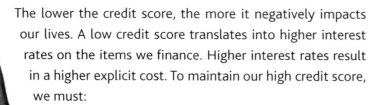

The lower the credit score, the more it negatively impacts our lives. A low credit score translates into higher interest rates on the items we finance. Higher interest rates result in a higher explicit cost. To maintain our high credit score, we must:

1. limit the amount of debt we have outstanding and available,

2. pay our bills on time, and most importantly,

3. *PAY OUR BILLS ON TIME!*

Many services will keep you informed of your current credit score. My credit card issuer keeps me updated on my credit score at no additional cost. I often see the advertisements for Credit Karma, a credit monitoring company. They advertise credit score information for free.

## Credit Card and Interest Rates

My parents were both born in the 1930s and married in 1950s. When they first married, the idea of a credit card was a foreign concept. If they wanted a big-ticket item, like a television, they had to have the discipline to save for it. Bank financing was limited to the purchase of cars and homes. If something was needed or desired beyond the budget, my parents had to save money from my dad's paycheck. I remember my mom telling me that she would put money aside in an envelope for a particular item.

The general-purpose credit card was born in the mid-1960s and gained tremendous popularity in the 1970s and has increased significantly since. As of September 2017, consumer credit card debt was over $900 billion, and the average household with credit card debt has balances totaling over $15,000.[3] Approximately 44 percent of all households carry some credit card debt as of December 2016.[4] The national average annual percentage rate (APR) for a new card just surpassed 16 percent as of July 2017.[5] The average household

with credit card debt pays over $900 in credit card interest per year.[6] In my book, $900 is a beach vacation!

The use of credit cards is not a bad thing. It allows for payment without having the cash readily available. A credit card is a tool, one of the many tools in our financial toolkit, and it provides a number of conveniences. I have two general purchase credit cards, in addition to a couple of store credit cards. I use my credit cards all the time. I only use cash for small purchases. I pay off my credit cards in full monthly and collect miles for travel or points for future discounts. I never carry a balance. I monitor my credit card use and don't spend more than I can pay off each month.

A credit card becomes a convenient cash alternative when we don't carry a balance. When we carry a balance, we have to be mindful that a credit card represents a loan with interest. We must be thoughtful about the APR at which we are borrowing and how long we expect the debt to be outstanding. The higher the APR and the longer the debt is outstanding, the higher the explicit cost. When we think about credit, we are essentially borrowing from future income, assuming that future income will be available to service the ever-increasing debt. Credit card debt can be a significant pitfall for many.

## Is buying something because it is on sale worth it if we have to purchase on credit and carry the balance forward?

I obtained my first credit card in college. The banks would come to campus and hand out applications to anyone and everyone. Of course, I applied immediately. With my new credit card, I had financial freedom. There are so many things I could now buy. It was especially pleasing when I purchased something on sale. I thought, *It's on sale, it fits, it looks good on me, and I don't have one like this, so it is meant for me.* But that discounted price is slowly chipped away by the accruing interest I had to pay. The actual cost is the price plus the interest. Depending on how long it would take me to pay off the item, the explicit cost could be the regular price or even higher. When I think about the cost of an item in those terms, is the purchase worth it? My engineering mind caused me to think long and hard about overindulgence on a credit card, thus curbing my behavior in the future, as it related to credit card usage.

YOU CAN WEAR THOSE NEW JEANS TONIGHT!

WHAT ABOUT THAT TRIP TO EUROPE? YOU ALWAYS WANTED TO PRACTICE YOUR FRENCH!

## Live and Learn

As I mentioned, I have been laid off twice in my career. I used credit cards to fund many expenses beyond my necessary household expenses, including unexpected purchases and car and home repairs. While unemployed, my furnace required a major repair; things happen at the most inconvenient times. With no heat, I wore a coat in my house for two days. I had no other choice but to put this repair on a credit card. Unfortunately, the longer I was unemployed, the more I would depend on my credit cards to live. I racked up some hefty credit card debt during this period.

Monthly, I would pay only the minimum required balance on time in an attempt to maintain a good credit score. I vowed to pay off all my credit card debt the first minute I secured a job. This life lesson taught me to put some security measures in place related to credit before an unfortunate situation arises, like unemployment. I suggest the following:

1. The credit cards that offer points, discounts, miles, and so on are typically not the cards with the lowest interest rates. Keep in your financial toolkit a credit card that has a low rate in case you have to carry a balance.

2. If you own a home, add to your financial toolkit a home equity line of credit (HELOC). A home equity line of credit is a loan that uses the equity in your home as collateral. Interest rates on credit cards are high, typically in the double digits. Current rates on a HELOC are in the mid-single digits. A HELOC is the cheapest form of credit for a consumer and can be used for anything. In hindsight, it would have been wiser to use a HELOC versus credit cards during my unemployment, but I did not have a HELOC in place when I unexpectedly lost my job. Please learn from my mistake. A note of caution with a HELOC, interest starts to accrue at the time of purchase and interest rates can be variable. Interest on a credit card begins to accrue after thirty days, and the interest rate is typically fixed.

I realize we are moving to a paperless society, but please review your credit card statement often. On the statement, it states how long it will take to pay off the current balance if only the minimum payment is made, and the total that will be paid over that period of time. If the outstanding balance is high coupled with a high interest rate, these figures can be shocking. Take, for example, a $5,000 outstanding balance with a 13% APR with a minimum payment of $50 (typically minimum payments are 1% of the outstanding balance). If only the minimum payment is made, it is estimated to take twenty-two years to pay off a total estimated cost of $10,000. Double the initial balance!

Credit is essential to how we function daily. It will impact how much we will pay for a house, a car, and other big-ticket items, and it can quite possibly affect our employment opportunities. I urge you to understand your credit score and take steps to improve it if necessary (a few suggestions follow shortly).

When it comes to credit cards, there is a multitude of choices, so shop around. If you know you will need to carry a balance, look for a card with the lowest APR and no annual fee. If you are not planning to carry a balance, then look for a card that provides the extra services and perks you seek. There are many choices for a credit card when you have a good credit score.

### Use Cash Instead of a Credit Card to Budget

Spending on a credit card can be easy. Often it doesn't feel like we are spending money until we receive the monthly bill that details all of our purchases. Cash is a great budgeting tool. Beyond those items like rent and utilities, which we typically pay with a check or via direct debit, use cash. Withdraw weekly the budgeted amount for weekly purchases. When cash is used, the impact of spending is much more real because you can see exactly what remains for the week in your wallet. Review purchases daily to stay on track for the week and ultimately for the month.

**We have many tools in our financial toolkit;
use the tools wisely and strategically to pave the path to
financial empow(er)ment. Take one small step each day!**

# To Do:

1. My credit score is _____

2. The annual percentage rate (APR) for my various credit cards are:

   _____

   _____

   _____

   _____

3. If the APR is high, contact the issuers of your current credit cards and try to negotiate lower rates.

4. If carrying a balance, transfer balances to a credit card with lower interest rate and no annual fees.

5. If you own a home, apply for a HELOC for unplanned expenses and possibly consolidate existing debt.

6. Pay more than the minimum payment whenever your budget allows.

If your debt is out of control, please seek help. Credit counseling services are available to assist. Check out your credit card statement. Contact information for counseling services is provided.

If your credit score is low, here are some suggestions to improve it:

$ Pay all of your bills on time.

$ Always pay at least the minimum on your credit cards by the due date.

$ Avoid increasing your available credit by applying for and opening new credit cards.

For additional tips, see "7 ways to improve your credit score" on Bankrate.com[7].

# Wealth vs. Stuff

**Stuff is not wealth!** Wealth is about amassing appreciating assets like stocks, bonds, real estate, etc., those items that have the potential to increase in value over time, appreciate. Our wealth (often referred to as net worth) equals the value of our assets minus the amount of our debt. Stuff is just stuff; stuff has little extrinsic long-term value. Stuff consists of depreciating assets, those items that lose value over time like clothing, furnishings, household items, etc. Sorry to break the news, but a car is a depreciating asset, so it falls in the "stuff" category. It is estimated that a new car loses 20 percent of its value in the first year of ownership. How can we create wealth when we are chipping away at our income with depreciating assets (stuff)?

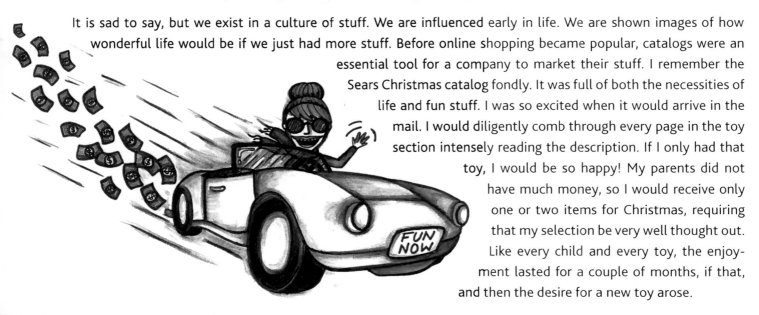

It is sad to say, but we exist in a culture of stuff. We are influenced early in life. We are shown images of how wonderful life would be if we just had more stuff. Before online shopping became popular, catalogs were an essential tool for a company to market their stuff. I remember the Sears Christmas catalog fondly. It was full of both the necessities of life and fun stuff. I was so excited when it would arrive in the mail. I would diligently comb through every page in the toy section intensely reading the description. If I only had that toy, I would be so happy! My parents did not have much money, so I would receive only one or two items for Christmas, requiring that my selection be very well thought out. Like every child and every toy, the enjoyment lasted for a couple of months, if that, and then the desire for a new toy arose.

Advertising is just not geared to children with their young and impressionable minds. We as adults are also lured into the images, even more so. The purpose of marketing and advertising should be to inform and educate consumers to make better decisions, but advertising has become very stylized, promoting images beyond the basic utility. We are constantly provided imagery of a utopian world. We begin to tell ourselves that life will be better if we had more stuff. Or at least we should have more stuff so that others can see us as accomplished and successful.

The goal of advertising is to wet our appetite to want more. The sixty-second advertisement with the focus on a single item is no longer enough. Advertising has become pervasive. Product placement has become highly prized during our entertainment hours and online searches. The new hour-long commercials are reality shows and celebrity news shows. And the newest platform—social media with Instagram, Twitter, etc.—allows for celebrity endorsements delivered directly to our smartphones.

We are shown glamorous lifestyles of which only a very small fraction of the population can afford, but many of us attempt to emulate. The designer items donned are well-placed items, at zero or minimum cost, of which we will pay full price if we purchase them. The advertiser wants to create desire so that we will part with our money. Nearly 70 percent of the gross domestic product (GDP) of the United States is consumer spending. We love our stuff! Consumerism seems to be the cornerstone of the American Dream. We want the largest house, the latest model car, the fabulous designer wardrobe, and the incredible dream vacation, creating a vision of what we think wealth looks like, often at the expense of lifelong indebtedness. Why do we fall for all the hype?

> "Buying is more American than thinking, and I'm as American as they come."
>
> —*Andy Warhol*

A house is an excellent investment. But it is not necessary to break the bank to get the largest home at the sacrifice of other aspects of wealth creation. Monthly we all have to pay to live somewhere, but total living expenses (that is, house, car, and associated expenses) should be limited to 50 percent of take-home pay. With the purchase of a house, we are paying toward something that we will eventually own, build equity in something tangible that can be used as collateral, realize significant appreciation if lucky, and hopefully have someplace to live rent-free in retirement.

An investment in a house (real estate) is the way to go as long as you do not create a situation in which you are *house poor*.[8] Square footage is nothing but a number if you cannot afford to appropriately furnish and maintain the space. In the world of real estate, the critical element is location, location, location; it's wise to own the smallest home in the best neighborhood. There's no need to overspend on a car. It is possible to be car poor, too. A car is a utility; we need a car for transportation. Purchase a car within budget, as a new car depreciates as soon as it is driven off the dealership lot, typically, as mentioned earlier, 20 percent in the first year.

Parting with our money has become much easier than ever before because we no longer have to get off of our comfortable couch to make a purchase; we can quickly pick up the phone or click *Buy Now*. It is so easy that shopping has become mindless. How often do we tell ourselves, *Just this one item and then no more?* Too often we are mindlessly purchasing stuff that we don't need. Once we remove the price tag, the value dramatically declines and a couple of months later the item is no longer top of mind.

I like stuff too, but we must focus on our goals. I am an advocate of putting "stuff" in the budget and titling it *discretionary spending*.

Remember, the happiness achieved when obtaining new stuff is temporary. The joy of having wealth is long term. Wealth is often not apparent. The neighbor or friend with the smallest house, the older model car, and the basic wardrobe can be the one with the most significant amount of wealth. The person with wealth does not feel the need to "keep up with the Joneses," as their asset portfolio provides peace of mind, self-fulfillment, and mental solace. When your budget allows (i.e., the discretionary spending component is abundant), buy all the stuff you want, and please do your part for the U.S. economy.

Liberate yourself from the need for an overabundance of stuff and focus on building wealth.

**You can do it!**

# To Do:

Before your next nonessential purchase, whether it be online or in-store, wait one day. Sleep on it. Spend a moment taking an inventory of what you currently have, and then ask yourself:

1. Am I making this purchase because I am feeling sad, bored, neglected, or deprived? If so, will the purchase provide a long-term remedy for the underlying feeling?

2. Will this purchase be a source of stress later because of the debt that has resulted?

3. Does my budget allow for this purchase? Have I completed my budget?

4. Am I forgoing a longer-term goal for immediate gratification?

# Create a Budget

**Here comes the hard part, budgeting.** Budgeting is the strategic tool that is essential in harnessing the daily discipline needed to be a good steward of your money. A budget will assist with financially navigating the **needs** of everyday life and creating a path to attaining your **wants**. Budgeting is very similar to being on a diet. Both take discipline. With a diet, you have to watch everything you eat. With a budget, you have to watch every dollar you spend. If you wish to be financially empow(**er**)ed, creating a budget and sticking to that budget is imperative. The budget is the tool that governs the flow of your money. It is the foundation on which your financial empow(**er**)ment exists.

**Let's create a budget!**

## Gross Income

Your gross income is your salary or wages earned from your job or your business. This would be the figure quoted as your salary.

### Pay Yourself First # 1—Retirement Savings

It is imperative that you contribute the maximum to an employer-sponsored savings plan annually. This contribution will be funded with pre-tax dollars, so your income is not taxed until after this contribution. Check with your employer; there may be other deductions you can take that are funded with pre-tax dollars, such as a commuter spending account, healthcare spending account (flexible spending account), child-care spending account, etc. The goal is to lower your taxable income.

### Take-Home Pay

Monthly take-home pay is monthly income less taxes and deductions. Taxes include federal, state, Social Security, Medicare, etc. The other deductions can vary. Your take-home pay is the dollars that are available to use to fund your daily living. Your budget will assist you with managing your day-to-day relationship with money. Let's examine your budget on a monthly basis:

**My monthly take home pay is: $_____**

***Pay Yourself First #2* (unplanned expenses): $_____** (deposit in savings account)

(Try your best to save 3 to 5 percent of monthly take-home pay for unplanned expenses. The goal should be to accumulate six months of living expenses as a cash reserve.)

## Expenses

There are host of financial obligations you have to maintain your lifestyle and standard of living. There are three broad categories: 1. annual expenses (*needs*), 2. monthly expenses (*needs*), which includes living expenses and monthly debt payments, and 3. discretionary spending (*wants or "stuff"*). Let's take a look at each:

### 1. Annual Expenses

Annual expenses are expenses you incur annually and semi-annually. These are obligations such as auto insurance (some are paid semi-annually), homeowner's insurance, and property taxes. (Homeowner's insurance and property taxes are sometimes included in the monthly mortgage payment.) Other annual expenses include memberships (i.e., health club and professional memberships if not paid monthly), subscriptions (i.e., magazine and trade publications), vehicle registrations, and scheduled maintenance on house and car.

My annual expenses are:

_____     _____

_____     _____

_____     _____

_____     _____

_____     _____

Divide your annual expenses by twelve to determine the monthly reserve you will put away for these expenses.

**Monthly reserve for my annual/semi-annual expenses: $_____**

## 2. Monthly Living Expenses

Think of food, shelter, and transportation—the essentials you need to live. Living expenses do not include dining out, entertainment, vacations, and new clothing. Think of these expenses as what you would be required to pay monthly if you lost your job. Ladies, I have included salon services and dry cleaning here.☺ I have been unemployed, and I know these services are important for securing your next opportunity, but they can be modified to include only essential services.

My monthly living expenses are:

| | | | |
|---|---|---|---|
| Rent/mortgage: | $_____ | Other transportation: | $_____ |
| Home utilities: | | (i.e., public transportation, cab, ride-sharing, parking, etc.) | |
|    Electricity: | $_____ | Dry cleaning: | $_____ |
|    Gas: | $_____ | Salon services: | $_____ |
|    Cable/WiFi: | $_____ | Child care: | $_____ |
|    Water/sewage: | $_____ | Pet care: | $_____ |
|    Garbage collection: | $_____ | Small miscellaneous purchases: | $_____ |
| Phone: | $_____ | Healthcare premiums/expenses: | $_____ |
| Car payment: | $_____ | Other: | $_____ |
| Gas/car wash: | $_____ | | $_____ |
| Groceries: | $_____ | | |
| (i.e., food, personal products, household cleaning supplies, etc.) | | **Total all of monthly living expenses:** | $_____ |

**My monthly expenses:** $_____

## Create a Budget

### Debt Obligations, Beyond House and Car

If you carry student loan debt, credit card debt, or any other type of revolving credit, you MUST pay your debt monthly to maintain an excellent credit score rating. At least pay the minimum amount required.

| | | | |
|---|---|---|---|
| Student loan: | $_____ | Credit card #3: | $_____ |
| Credit card #1: | $_____ | Other: | $_____ |
| Credit card #2: | $_____ | Other: | $_____ |

**My minimum monthly debt obligation is: $_____**

## 3. Discretionary Spending

Here is the calculation to determine what's left for discretionary spending on your **wants.**

| | |
|---|---|
| **Monthly take-home pay:** | $_____ |
| Minus *pay yourself first* (savings-unplanned expenses): | $_____ |
| Minus monthly reserve for annual expenses (needs): | $_____ |
| Minus monthly expenses (needs): | $_____ |
| Minus minimum monthly debt obligations: | $_____ |
| **Equals Discretionary Spending on *wants*:** | $_____ |

If all your *needs* and debt obligations are satisfied and you have allocated appropriately to build your cash reserve, you can move on to your *wants*!

## The Reality

Regardless of whether or not there is a positive number for discretionary spending, we all have *wants*. It is impossible not to have *wants*. *Wants* include entertainment, dining out, clothing, gifts, vacations, etc. Your *wants* will further compound your debt when discretionary spending is zero or negative. Review some of the larger items in your budget, which are typically housing and transportation and attempt to make adjustments.

A good guideline for budgeting of your take-home pay is the "50/30/20 rule," coined by U.S. Senator, author, and Harvard scholar specializing in bankruptcy law, Elizabeth Warren. It works like this:

**50% Needs (Living Expenses) / 30% Wants /
20% Debt Obligations and Savings**

## Budget Tips

Just as there are trade-offs in life, there are trade-offs in your budget, especially if you want to allocate more money to discretionary spending. We need the food and basic utilities to live, but certain aspects of daily living offer some wiggle room. Here are some ideas:

$ Keep your thermostat low in the winter and higher in the summer. I don't mind wearing a sweater around the house, and I enjoy snuggling under my blankets at night in the winter. In the summer, I have a ceiling fan over my bed to cool my bedroom at night.

## Create a Budget

$ Cable TV can be very costly, especially if premium channels are included. Be selective with the channels you choose and investigate less expensive streaming options. I was able to cut my cable bill by more than half by opting for a streaming service.

$ Purchasing lunch daily is much more expensive than bringing lunch from home. Homemade coffee is far less cost prohibitive than coffee shop purchases. I keep teabags in my desk drawer and always have a refillable water bottle.

$ Limit restaurant dinners. Make dining out a special occasion and not a regular activity. Additionally, the alcoholic drinks in a restaurant can be as much as or more than the appetizer, and, in some cases, as much as an entrée. Limiting your consumption of alcoholic beverages will help save on the final dining bill.

$ The latest model smartphone is not a *need* if your current phone is working. These days, the cost of a new phone is the same price as a vacation. For Christmas 2017, I purchased a new Galaxy Note8 utilizing a two-for-one promotion with my uncle. I was upgrading from a Galaxy Note 3. Needless to say, the latest model phone is not a priority of mine.

$ When it comes to furniture, cars, and housing, try not to rent/lease when buying is an option. When you purchase an item, it is yours forever. Buy used if buying new is not in the budget. I purchased my first new car and my first house at twenty-five years old. This new car purchase would be the only new car I would ever buy. I understand that a new car depreciates once it is driven off the dealership's lot. Every vehicle I have bought since then has been used.

Only *you* can determine if the trade-off is worth it, but when you want a new item that is not in your budget or an unexpected expense occurs, remind yourself of all the things you could have done to lower your monthly bills. Is the stress worth it?

Before you charge ahead and purchase a substantial amount of new *stuff*, review your debt position. If you have debt outstanding, I strongly encourage you to pay off your debt as soon as possible. As I mentioned, I apply extra to my mortgage whenever possible. Also, ensure that you have a comfortable amount in your savings account.

Additionally, you will want to protect your wealth. Healthcare insurance is extremely critical. Healthcare expense is the number one reason for personal bankruptcy in the United States[9]. The majority of those filing for bankruptcy, as the result of medical expenses, had some form of medical insurance. Contrary to popular belief, medical expense bankruptcy extends beyond those that are uninsured. Please check that you are adequately insured.

**Now it is time to enjoy life and enjoy the fruits of your labor. You have earned it!**

# Conclusion

Life is a journey to be enjoyed. You should be happy along the way. We are happier when we achieve the goals we set for ourselves. Often our financial situation becomes an impediment to pursuing a business idea or new job opportunity. Don't allow poor financial planning to derail your dreams. Write your own story. Live your personal story that is uniquely yours, not someone else's.

Throughout my life, I have never been overly frugal because I like nice things, but I always make purchases with an eye toward value. My goal has always been to live on less than my take-home pay and save for the unplanned expense and occurrences of life because sh*t happens. I determine the things that are important to me and occasionally splurge on items and activities that will bring me utter joy. I continually think best how my hard-earned dollars should be spent. I have never wanted to endure the stress of being flat broke, and thankfully I haven't been.

In general, ladies, we are behind the curve as it relates to having a long-term financial plan. We are leaders and role models in our households, in our communities, and at work. And we need to take the lead and become role models as it relates to personal financial security. It is up to us to make the changes needed to become financially more empow(**er**)ed. Look at your daily spending and saving behavior to ensure you are where you need to be.

# Five Financial Empow(er)ment Strategies for the Savvy Gal

1. Make goals and stay focused. Create a vision board and look at it every morning so that you can stay focused throughout the day. Keep one or two of the images in your wallet so that when you are making a purchase, you have a friendly reminder of what you are striving for.

2. Save continuously both for retirement and unplanned life events. The stress of a devastating financial situation cannot be avoided if you have no money in the bank, even if you are impeccably dressed. Start early, so that the amount you wish to save monthly is not onerous and debilitating.

3. A credit card is a financial tool, not a life raft. A credit card is not meant to keep you afloat but to assist with navigating the water. When you purchase items on a credit card and you are unable to pay the balance, you are essentially kicking a financial obligation down the road. If you continue to grow the balance, you are relying on future income that might not be guaranteed. Also, you are paying more than the stated price for a depreciating item. Credit card spending is easy; instead use cash for daily purchases and only keep on hand what you have budgeted for the week.

4. Focus on building wealth and not on buying stuff. The thrill of a new item is short lived, but the comfort of wealth is long lasting. Don't fall for the hype! Analyze your spending on nonessential items. Is the purchase rooted in pure emotion such as neglect, sadness, or boredom? Will this purchase be a source of stress later because of the debt that has resulted? Will you have to forgo a larger aspiration as the result of this purchase? Stay focused on what is important to you.

5. Like diets, budgets can be challenging, but once you incorporate healthy financial habits into your routine, it becomes mindless. Modify your financial appetite accordingly. Build balance into your budget, so that you can address your *needs* with ease and quickly move on to your *wants*. The *wants* are so much more fun!

Your financial security is up to you.
Others don't empow(er) you, you empow(er) yourself.

**Inner strength** leads to **outer success**.

# APPENDIX:
# Basic Terms of Investing

**A long-term savings plan offered by your employer** or an IRA will be the first encounter most people will have with regard to making an investment decision. This appendix is intended to provide you with a primer of fundamental investment terms, which is the first step to understanding basic investment strategies. This part of the book is purely definitional and provides some examples. This is only the tip of the iceberg, so please do further research. Now, hold on to your hat, here we go!

The **Capital Market** (aka **"The Market"**) is a financial system in which capital assets such as **equity** and **debt** are traded. The Capital Market brings buyers and sellers together to trade financial assets.

**Stock** represents *ownership* in an entity, which is often referred to as **equity.** For example, if you give your friend Nicole money for her new business XYZ, and in exchange, she considers you a part owner of XYZ, you have an equity interest in XYZ. As part owner, you will participate in the potential profit and success of XYZ. You will also be subjected to the loss of your investment if Nicole proves to be unsuccessful and abandons her business. In the case of the investment in XYZ, where the stock of XYZ is not publicly traded, your investment would be characterized as **private**

equity. Nicole's private company XYZ would initiate an **initial public offering** (**IPO**) to become publicly traded on a public exchange. Once Nicole's company XYZ becomes public, and its **stock** is traded on the public exchange, any investor can now purchase **stock** in XYZ. No longer is the investment of XYZ just limited to the friends and family of Nicole or private investors.

**Public equities** are traded on exchanges such as the NYSE, NASDAQ, and AMEX. The **New York Stock Exchange** (**NYSE**) is a stock exchange based in New York City that is considered the largest equities-based exchange in the world. Other exchanges are the **National Association of Securities Dealers Automated Quotation System** (**NAS-DAQ**) and the **American Stock Exchange** (**AMEX**).

## Appendix: Basic Terms of Investing

A **bond** represents a *debt* obligation (i.e., loan) owed to you by an entity. This is often referred to as **fixed income**. For example, if you lend your friend Karen money for her new business ABC, and Karen agrees to pay you back with interest, you hold a **bond** in ABC. It is called **fixed income** because the interest you receive from the loan is often at a fixed rate. Even if Karen is wildly successful, the interest paid to you will be the interest you initially agreed to; it is fixed. Most publicly traded **bonds** are *not* traded via exchanges like stocks, but rather are traded over the counter (OTC). **OTC** is a decentralized market where market participants trade between each other.

**Risk vs. return**—The more **risk** you take, the higher the expected **return** on your investment.

**Risk tolerance**—How much risk can you "emotionally" accept? What amount of **volatility** (up-and-down movement) will cause you to lose sleep? If the market movement up and down causes you stress, then you are **risk adverse**. If the market movements up and down do not cause stress, then you are a **risk seeker**. Your tolerance for risk will determine your allocation to riskier assets in your portfolio.

**Time horizon**—The length of time you have to invest until you will need to liquidate your investment. Conventional wisdom would dictate that the longer you have to invest, the more **risk** you can take. For example, Michelle (age 25) and Joni (age 55) are both saving for retirement. Both are expecting to retire at age 65. Michelle has a longer time horizon than Joni, as Michelle will not retire for forty years, whereas Joni will be retiring in ten years. Michelle can take more risk with her investments than Joni.

## BOND SPECIFICS

**Bond maturity date**—The date at which the borrower (in the above example, Karen) agrees to pay the original borrowed amount and any applicable interest.

**Years to maturity** are the years until the original principal amount and applicable interest is returned to the investor. Explained another way, how long do you want to lend your money: short term, intermediate term, or long term? You may want to buy a boat in a couple of years, so you will only lend for two years (**short-term bond**); you may want to build your dream house in eight years, so you will only lend for eight years (**intermediate-term bond**); or you may want to save for retirement, so you lend for thirty years (**long-term bond**). The longer the length until maturity of the bond, the higher the expected return because the probability of **default** (not paying the loan) is higher. For example, if you loan money to Karen for thirty years, the probability of default is higher as something negative could happen to Karen or her business over such a long period of time. The expected return is higher because there exists more risk.

## TYPES OF BONDS

The type of bond depends upon to whom you lend your money. Do you wish to lend to a corporation (**corporate bond**) or to the government (**treasury or agency bond**)? **Treasury bonds** are often referred to as **risk-free bonds** because it is assumed that the government will not default on its debt. Given that corporate bonds are considered riskier than government bonds, you would expect a higher return from a corporate bond.

**Municipal bonds** are bonds issued by states, cities, counties, and other governmental entities.

All corporate bonds and municipal bonds are rated. Highly rated corporate bonds are considered **investment grade.** A low-rated bond is considered **non-investment grade** or a **junk bond**. **Junk bonds** have a higher default rate. Some investors like junk bonds because the interest rate is high, although the risk of default is higher. The higher the risk, the higher the expected return.

## RISK—STOCK VS. BONDS

**Stocks** are riskier than **bonds**. Also, **stocks** are more volatile than **bonds**, as the value of your investment will fluctuate more often in a more acute fashion. In the earlier example, the equity investment in XYZ is much riskier than the fixed-income investment in ABC, so an investor would expect to receive a higher return in XYZ. The investor who takes more risk expects to get compensated with higher returns.

## INDEX/BENCHMARK

An **index** is a basket of securities (stocks or bonds) with a particular set of characteristics. The S&P 500 **index** is an index of 500 widely held publicly traded U.S. stocks. There are several **indices.** An **index** is used to observe a broad market segment, economic sector, geography, etc., and is used to benchmark performance of a mutual fund or exchange traded fund (ETF). **Russell** and **S&P** (Standard & Poor's) are widely used and recognized U.S. equity indices. Morgan Stanley Capital International (**MSCI**) is the market leader in global equity indices. **Bloomberg Barclay** is the global market leader in fixed income indexing. There are several indices; too many to list. When you invest in a mutual fund, the corresponding benchmark/index will be provided.

## ACTIVE MANAGEMENT

**Mutual fund**—Professional management of a collection of stocks or bonds. The benefit of investing in a mutual fund is that it is under professional management and the expectation that the management of the fund will outperform the benchmark plus fees. Every mutual fund has a stated strategy. And, as an investor, you are investing in a fund to gain exposure to that stated strategy (i.e., large-cap, mid-cap, small-cap, growth, value, U.S., non-U.S., emerging markets, technology, healthcare, financials, industrials, etc.).

Here's an example: You attend your high school reunion, and you discover that over fifty of your former classmates have thriving businesses in a variety of industries. What luck! And their companies are all publicly traded. Instead of investing directly with each one of your former classmates individually, you happen to have a neighbor Joy who manages a **mutual fund** that just happens to invest in 100 stocks, including the stocks of the companies of all your former classmates. It is much more efficient to invest in the mutual fund managed by Joy instead of investing in all those stocks individually. You can invest a small amount of money with Joy as Joy pools your investment with that of other investors. And by investing in Joy's mutual fund, your investment is more diversified because Joy is not only investing the stock of your fifty friends but fifty other stocks, thus providing you with diversification.

Additionally, Joy is a professional, so she is monitoring your investment, ensuring that the stocks she invests in are following their stated strategy. Because Joy is monitoring all the stocks she holds, you are confident that Joy will sell a stock if fundamentals change and become negative and purchase a new stock if she researches and discovers a new stock that has positive fundamentals. Joy is an **active** mutual fund manager.

How do you know if Joy is a good or bad mutual fund manager? The performance of Joy's fund is measured against a **benchmark** or **index.** The performance of every mutual fund is compared to its stated benchmark or index. Joy is an **active** manager, so her goal is to outperform the benchmark index over a market cycle. Joy would inform you of her specific strategy when she discusses her mutual fund with you. Also, she will inform you which **index** she will use to **benchmark** the performance of her mutual fund. She cannot change the index unless she informs you and all investors prior to making the change.

## PASSIVE MANAGEMENT

Your friend Pat is a **passive** manager, so her goal is to invest in every stock in the **benchmark/index**. This means her goal is just to replicate the performance of the **benchmark/index**. The fees you pay Pat would be less than the fees you pay Joy.

An **Exchange Traded Fund (ETF)** is a marketable security and trades like a stock. It tracks a specific benchmark/index. Like a stock the price of an **ETF** fluctuates throughout the day. An **ETF** is an alternate form of passive management.

Mutual funds (valued at the end of the day) can be passively managed in addition to ETFs (traded like a stock—intraday pricing).

## U.S. STOCK MARKET SEGMENTATION

Market capitalization equals the number of shares outstanding multiplied by the current market price.

**Large capitalization** (often referred to as **large-cap** stocks) are stocks with a market-cap greater than $10 billion. An index that would represent these stocks would be the S&P 500, Russell 1000, or DJIA. For example, Amazon, Facebook, Exxon Mobil, and JPMorgan Chase are **large-cap** stocks.

**Mid-capitalization** (often referred to as **mid-cap** stocks) are stocks with a market cap between $2 and $10 billion. An index that would represent these stocks would be S&P MidCap 400 or Russell 2500. For example, Domino's Pizza, JetBlue Airlines, Dunkin' Brands, and Wendy's are **mid-cap** stocks.

**Small capitalization** (often referred to as **small-cap** stocks) are stocks with a market cap less than $2 billion. An index that would represent these stocks would be S&P SmallCap 600 or Russell 2000. For example, Guess, DSW, LendingTree, and Stamps.com are **small-cap** stocks.

There are several **economic sectors** in which an investor can specifically invest, including technology, telecommunications, healthcare, consumer discretionary, consumer staples, financials, industrials, materials, energy, and utilities, just to name a few. For example, my friend Kim retired from her job in the healthcare industry and is now a professional mutual fund manager. She will specifically invest in stock in the **healthcare** industry. Kim is a **sector-specific** active mutual fund manager, as she is knowledgeable about the healthcare industry.

## Appendix: Basic Terms of Investing

### INVESTING INTERNATIONALLY

The **international** equity markets can be broadly divided into **International Developed, International Emerging**, and **International Frontier** markets. As mentioned earlier, **MSCI** is the market leader in maintaining global equity market indices in which international mutual funds and ETFs can be benchmarked against.

Per the **MSCI ACWI** (All Country World Index), which captures equity returns of 23 developed countries and 24 emerging countries, the U.S. only represents approximately 52% of the index (as of December 2017). If an investor only invests in the U.S. equity market, then the investor is only investing in half the global equity opportunity set.

If you were to invest in a mutual fund that invests stocks in the **International Developed** markets, the mutual fund would hold stocks of companies that are domiciled in countries and on continents with developed economies such as Europe, Australia, Japan, Hong Kong, U.K., Singapore, etc.

If you were to invest in a mutual fund that invests stocks in the **International Emerging** markets, the mutual fund would hold stocks of companies that are domiciled in countries with emerging economies such as Russia, China, Mexico, India, Indonesia, South Korea, etc.

If you were to invest in a mutual fund that invests stocks in the **International Frontier** markets, the mutual fund would hold stocks of companies that are domiciled in countries with emerging economies such as Kenya, Bangladesh, Croatia, Argentina, Sri Lanka, etc.

Here is an example: If you wanted to invest in a mutual fund that invests in Samsung, you could either invest in an **International Emerging** market mutual fund because Samsung is domiciled in South Korea, or a Global Technology sector-specific mutual fund because it is a technology company.

### DIVERSIFICATION

Portfolio **Diversification**—Investing in a variety of strategies, segments, and geographies. On average, returns are expected to be greater and risk reduced over a market cycle versus investing in a single strategy, segment, or geography.

**Target Date Fund (TDF)**—A diversified fund, comprised of several mutual funds, typically invested in both stocks and bonds with a variety of strategies, segments, and geographies. A **TDF** is designed to provide a single investment solution. The allocation of the **TDF** begins risky (more allocation to equity investments) and becomes more conservative (more allocation to fixed income investment) as the target date approaches. This is also referred to as an age-based fund.

# Notes

# References

1. The Balance—How Much Home Can You Afford? Mortgage Rule of Thumb https://www.thebalance.com/how-much-home-can-you-afford-mortgage-rule-of-thumb-1289846. Accessed 3/21/2018.

2. https://www.irs.gov/retirement-plans/plan-participant-employee/retirement-topics-contributions

3. NerdWallet—2017 American Household Credit Card Debt Study. https://www.nerdwallet.com/blog/average-credit-card-debt-household/. Accessed 3/20/18.

4. Ibid.

5. CreditCards.com – Rate Survey. https://www.creditcards.com/credit-card-news/interest-rate-report-120617-unchanged-2121.php. Accessed 3/20/18.

6. NerdWallet—2017 American Household Credit Card Debt Study. https://www.nerdwallet.com/blog/average-credit-card-debt-household/. Accessed 3/20/18.

7. Bankrate.com "7 ways to improve your credit score" https://www.bankrate.com/finance/debt/7-simple-ways-improve-credit-score-1.aspx. Accessed 3/21/2018.

8. "House poor is a situation that describes a person who spends a large proportion of his or her total income on home ownership including mortgage payments, property taxes, maintenance and utilities. House poor individuals are short of cash for discretionary items and tend to have trouble meeting other financial obligations." —Investopedia.com, "House Poor." Accessed 3/20/18.

9. Investopedia—Top 5 Reasons Why People Go Bankrupt. https://www.investopedia.com/financial-edge/0310/top-5-reasons-people-go-bankrupt.aspx. Accessed 4/18/18.

# About the Author

**Beth Burns** is a financial empow(er)ment coach, speaker, workshop facilitator, and motivational author, inspiring both women and men to be better stewards of their money. She earned a BS in engineering at Michigan State University and an MBA from the University of Chicago. She has held various positions in the investments sector throughout her career, including mergers and acquisitions, investor relations, portfolio management, and investment management consulting.

In 2012, she launched *the (er) factor* and trademarked its accompanying catchphrase, *(er) is in her...find your (er) inside*®. The mission of *the (er) factor* is to inspire women to seek happiness inside themselves. Women are happier when they achieve the goals they set for themselves; feel healthy in body, mind, and spirit; feel empowered to take on any challenge; exhibit mental tenacity and strength; and approach decision-making with wisdom.

In 2017, Beth published her first book *Inner Strength, Outer Success—Practical strategies to being happi(er), healthi(er), empow(er)ed, strong(er), and wis(er)*. While speaking and coaching others, Beth surmised that many were facing financial challenges. To that end, Beth was determined to write a book to address financial empow(er)ment specifically. With *Inner Strength, Outer Success—A savvy gal's guide to financial empow(er)ment*, Beth assists readers in enhancing their daily relationship with money, as inner strength leads to outer success and ultimate happiness.

Visit Beth Burns at www.innerstrengthoutersuccess.com.

Made in the USA
Columbia, SC
24 March 2019